SAVE
AMERICA
PRESIDENT DONALD J. TRUMP
TEXT OHIO TO 88022
Fake News
I0814785

Fake News

Heidi Newbauer

Living in AMERICA

CREATIVE EDUCATION
CREATIVE PAPERBACKS

Published by Creative Education and Creative Paperbacks
P.O. Box 227, Mankato, Minnesota 56002
Creative Education and Creative Paperbacks are imprints of The Creative Company
www.thecreativecompany.us

Book design by Graham Morgan (www.bluedes.com)
Art direction by Tom Morgan
Edited by Jill Kalz

Images by Getty (Bettmann, FilippoBacci, Hollie Adams, Keystone, Keystone-France, Photo12, Shawn Thew/EPA/Bloomberg, Tayfun Coskun/Anadolu Agency, The Washington Post, Universal History Archive, zhengshun tang), Pexels (Terje Sollie), Unsplash (Gian Cescon), Wikimedia Commons (Art Young, Byron H. Rollins, Jamie Kelso~commonswiki, John Boyd, John Dunlap, Library of Congress, LiteraryCritic1, L. M. Glackens, Michael Vadon, National Museum of the U.S. Navy, SS Main Office)

Library of Congress Cataloging-in-Publication Data
Names: Newbauer, Heidi, author.
Title: Fake news / Heidi Newbauer.
Description: Mankato : Creative Education and Creative Paperbacks, 2025. | Series: Living in America | Includes bibliographical references and index. | Audience: Ages 10–14 | Audience: Grades 7–9 | Summary: "A social studies title for young adults that examines the history of fake news across media in the United States of America and its ties to COVID-19 and Donald Trump. Includes sidebars, real-person profiles, a glossary, a timeline, and further resources"—Provided by publisher.
Identifiers: LCCN 2023047187 (print) | LCCN 2023047188 (ebook) | ISBN 9781640269088 (library binding) | ISBN 9781682774588 (paperback) | ISBN 9798889890768 (ebook)
Subjects: LCSH: Fake news—Juvenile literature. | Journalism—United States—History—21st century—Juvenile literature.
Classification: LCC PN4888.F35 N49 2025 (print) | LCC PN4888.F35 (ebook) | DDC 070.430973—dc23/eng/20231106
LC record available at https://lccn.loc.gov/2023047187
LC ebook record available at https://lccn.loc.gov/2023047188

Printed in China

CONTENTS

Introduction

It was November 2, 1920—Election Day in the United States. Radio station KDKA announced that presidential candidate Warren G. Harding had won the election over his competitor, James M. Cox. The announcement marked the start of a new presidency, but it also marked the start of **broadcast news** on the radio. For the first time in U.S. history, people *heard* the news before they could read it in the newspaper.

On November 9, 2016, ABC News announced over a television livestream that presidential candidate Donald J. Trump had won the election over his competitor, Hilary Rodham Clinton. Nearly 100 years after the Harding/Cox results, *this* news was broadcast not only in newspapers and over TV and radio but also on the Internet. Social **media** blew up. Within seconds, news of

Radio broadcast equipment in the 1920s was incredibly big and bulky.

U.S. president Donald J. Trump often claimed that unfavorable coverage of his conduct or statements, even if proven true, was "fake news."

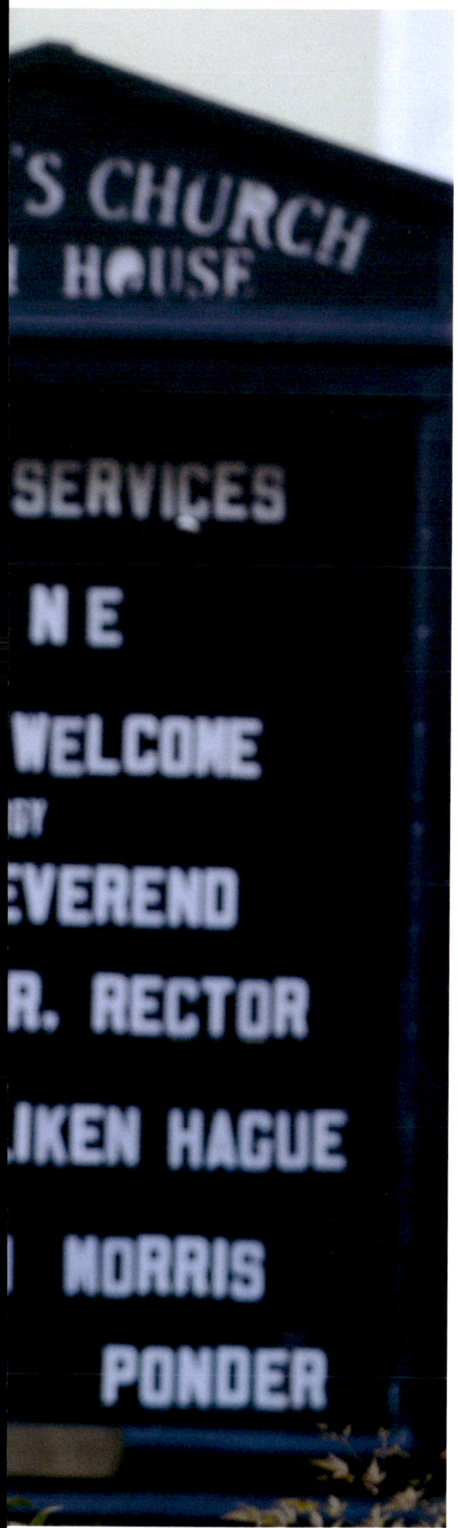

the election reached millions of smartphones, tablets, and other electronic devices across the nation.

Americans have relied on the media for their news for hundreds of years. They have trusted journalists, publishers, and announcers to tell them the truth about the world around them. But as technology has improved and media outlets have grown, **fake news** has become a huge concern.

Falsehoods have always existed in media, but 2016 marked a turning point. President Trump and others embraced the term "fake news." They used it often, usually whenever reporting cast them in an unfavorable light. As the term spread, people became increasingly confused about what to believe and from whom. Fake news looked like "real news," so how could Americans tell the difference?

Poisoned At The Source

CHAPTER 1:

Newspapers and Radio

In the earliest **colonial** days, before the United States was officially a country, people often shared news by word of mouth. Official documents created by the government were read aloud to townspeople. The lowest social classes tended to not be able to read or write, so they relied on town criers for their news. It was easy for news to be reshaped and spread inaccurately, especially if it hadn't been heard firsthand.

In the 1700s, **literacy** rates in the colonies increased, and printed media grew. Pamphlets, newsletters, and longer newspapers began to circulate widely. The first newspaper was *The New England Courant*, which appeared as a weekly in 1721. It was run by the brother of Benjamin Franklin, one of the Founding Fathers of the United States. By 1775, there were 37 newspapers in circulation. Many of them included gossip columns, which pushed the idea of opinion as fact.

By the 20th century, corner newstands were a common place for Americans to learn about local and world events.

2 DAILY MIRROR 2

The Pennſylvania Packet, *and Daily Advertiſer.*

[Price Four-Pence.] WEDNESDAY, September 19, 1787. [No. 2690.]

WE, the People of the United States, in order to form a more perfect Union, eſtabliſh Juſtice, inſure domeſtic Tranquility, provide for the common Defence, promote the General Welfare, and ſecure the Bleſſings of Liberty to Ourſelves and our Poſterity, do ordain and eſtabliſh this Conſtitution for the United States of America.

ARTICLE I.

Sect. 1. ALL legiſlative powers herein granted ſhall be veſted in a Congreſs of the United States, which ſhall conſiſt of a Senate and Houſe of Repreſentatives.

Sect. 2. The Houſe of Repreſentatives ſhall be compoſed of members choſen every ſecond year by the people of the ſeveral ſtates, and the electors in each ſtate ſhall have the qualifications requiſite for electors of the moſt numerous branch of the ſtate legiſlature.

No perſon ſhall be a repreſentative who ſhall not have attained to the age of twenty-five years, and been ſeven years a citizen of the United States, and who ſhall not, when elected, be an inhabitant of that ſtate in which he ſhall be choſen.

Repreſentatives and direct taxes ſhall be apportioned among the ſeveral ſtates which may be included within this Union, according to their reſpective numbers, which ſhall be determined by adding to the whole number of free perſons, including thoſe bound to ſervice for a term of years, and excluding Indians not taxed, three-fifths of all other perſons. The actual enumeration ſhall be made within three years after the firſt meeting of the Congreſs of the United States, and within every ſubſequent term of ten years, in ſuch manner as they ſhall by law direct. The number of repreſentatives ſhall not exceed one for every thirty thouſand, but each ſtate ſhall have at leaſt one repreſentative; and until ſuch enumeration ſhall be made, the ſtate of New-Hampſhire ſhall be entitled to chuſe three, Maſſachuſetts eight, Rhode-Iſland and Providence Plantations one, Connecticut five, New-York ſix, New-Jerſey four, Pennſylvania eight, Delaware one, Maryland ſix, Virginia ten, North-Carolina five, South-Carolina five, and Georgia three.

When vacancies happen in the repreſentation from any ſtate, the Executive authority thereof ſhall iſſue writs of election to fill ſuch vacancies.

The Houſe of Repreſentatives ſhall chuſe their Speaker and other officers; and ſhall have the ſole power of impeachment.

Sect. 3. The Senate of the United States ſhall be compoſed of two ſenators from each ſtate, choſen by the legiſlature thereof, for ſix years; and each ſenator ſhall have one vote.

ZOOM IN: THE FIRST DAILY

The first successful daily newspaper in the United States was the *Pennsylvania Packet and Daily Advertiser*. It began on September 21, 1784. About three years later, on September 19, 1787, the paper had the honor of being the first newspaper to publish a copy of the U.S. Constitution. The Constitution had been approved, or ratified, just two days earlier. The publisher of the *Packet* was John Dunlap. He was an Irish immigrant who had come to America in 1757 to learn the printing trade from his uncle. By 1776, Dunlap was an official printer to the federal government.

Fake news can be intentionally false. In this case, there is usually a motive behind it, one that benefits the person or group spreading the falsehood. Fake news was already alive and well by the time the United States declared its independence. In 1782, Franklin created a fake issue of the *Boston Newspaper* to build support for the American Revolution (1774–83). The paper claimed that the British government had hired American Indians to kill soldiers and civilians. The false information spread quickly to other newspapers. It boosted support for the new nation and increased public hatred toward American Indians.

In 1835, the *New York Sun* ran reports of animal-like creatures living on the moon. Today, people know this was clearly fake news. But in the early 1800s, long before humans stepped foot on the moon in 1969, readers believed it. Circulation numbers for the *Sun* shot from 8,000 to 19,000, making it the best-selling newspaper of the time. The "Great Moon **Hoax**" was nothing more than a business strategy to draw in more readers.

Much of the time, the purpose of fake news is to discredit something or someone. It is used to change others' opinions and beliefs. In 1844, anti-Catholic newspapers in Philadelphia, Pennsylvania, falsely accused Irish Catholics of robbing schools and stealing Bibles. They also played into anti-immigrant feelings held by some people in the community. The false reports fueled violent attacks on Catholic churches. Buildings burned, and several people were killed or wounded.

During World War I (1914–18), a rumor spread about a German "corpse factory." Several different newspapers from around the world, including the United States, falsely claimed

The Pennsylvania Packet and Daily Advertiser **published a copy of the U.S. Constitution soon after it was approved in 1787.**

ZOOM IN: BIG FLASH, LITTLE SUBSTANCE

"Yellow journalism" is a term that grew out of competition in the 1890s. There were two rival newspaper tycoons named Joseph Pulitzer and William Randolph Hearst. Each man wanted his paper to be the most-read newspaper in New York City. Pulitzer's *New York World* was the most popular in New York until Hearst came along and bought *The Journal*. The two New York papers featured cartoons to discredit each other. **Sensationalism** became common practice and affected journalism across the country.

that the German military was removing fat from dead soldiers. They said the fat was being used to make soap, food for animals, and other materials. Ten years later, a British general admitted that he had made up the story. He had wanted to get Chinese leaders to join the war against Germany.

The news in newspapers today is often outdated by the time the papers are delivered, thanks to social media and 24-hour news broadcasts. However, even with constant media availability, a news story still takes time to develop.

Fake news can be the result of **circular reasoning**, which is also called circular reporting. This type of news reporting happens when a fact is not proven but is considered true based on what others have said about it. This can be a good thing. For example, a parent tells their child that the best way to shoot a basketball is with a certain snap of the wrist. This advice is based on what the coaches have shown both the parent and the child. The child

Sensationalism in newspapers resulted in more interest and sales but also more concern about truth in reporting.

would be wise to try and shoot the basketball that way because it's advice from experts, the coaches.

Circular reasoning becomes a problem when different websites or newspapers run a fake news story, others pick it up, and then each outlet cites the other as a verified source. For example, Site 1 and Site 2 run a story about the birth of a three-headed cow. Site 3 picks up the story and says, "According to Sites 1 and 2, a three-headed cow was born." The "fact" isn't proven, but it appears to be true because two other sources mentioned it. This is one way in which fake news can spread like wildfire.

After broadcast news debuted on American radio in 1920, listeners tuned in regularly to hear the latest headlines. Shows such as President Franklin D. Roosevelt's *Fireside Chats* became extremely popular. Later, during World War II (1939–45), trusted

Through his *Fireside Chats* radio program in the 1930s, President Franklin D. Roosevelt became a trusted and comforting presence in the United States.

journalists such as Edward R. Murrow and Walter Cronkite delivered live broadcasts from the front lines. The 1930s and 1940s were known as the "Golden Age of Radio" in the United States.

Sometimes, fake news happens by accident. Such was the case on October 30, 1938. Orson Welles presented a radio adaptation of the H. G. Wells science fiction novel *The War of the Worlds*. Before the story of flesh-eating monsters from Mars began, Wells gave a disclaimer. He told the audience that the show was *not* based on real events. It was *not* news coverage.

The radio show was a huge hit. However, many listeners tuned in late and missed the disclaimer. They thought the adaptation was actual news. They believed Martians were attacking the country. Terrified, around 20 percent of the listening audience panicked. They called their local police, newspapers, and radio stations, wondering what to do. Some newspaper publishers took advantage of the confusion. They ran headlines the next day such as "Attack from Mars in Radio Play Puts Thousands in Fear" and "Radio Fake Scares Nation." What started as a story meant for entertainment turned into fake news.

MUTUAL

CHAPTER 2:

Rise of Propaganda

The spreading of information or ideas to persuade people, to convince them to do or believe in something, is called **propaganda**. It can be as small as a pamphlet seeking members for a neighborhood book club. It can be as powerful as posters calling for the elimination of an entire race.

When the World War I peace treaty was signed in 1919, winning countries wanted to punish Germany. They wanted it to take full responsibility for the war. Terms were harsh. They required Germany to give up territory, disarm and shrink its military, and pay an enormous sum (about $423 billion in 2019 dollars). The German economy suffered. The government became unstable. Many Germans, who felt they had been treated unfairly by the treaty, were angry. It was

Newspapers, radio, and film allowed leaders such as Germany's Adolf Hitler to bring propaganda into the daily lives of their nations' citizens.

during this time that a man named Adolf Hitler rose in the ranks and became leader of the Nazi Party. He started blaming Germany's fall and resulting troubles on one group of people: the Jews.

Support for Hitler's ideas grew stronger as frustrated post-war Germans continued to struggle to make ends meet. After Hitler claimed power as the Chancellor of Germany in 1933, propaganda pamphlets, newspapers, and radio shows began to appear. They warned that Jewish people were a dangerous threat to the success of a new and improved German nation. Some posters showed Jewish men as ugly monsters out to drink the blood of German children. Carnival parades featured floats with Jewish dummies hanging from rope nooses. One German newspaper, *Der Stürmer* ("The Attacker"), issued this headline: "The Jews Are Our Misfortune."

Stereotypes of Jewish people have existed for centuries, just as stereotypes of Black people, Asian people, and countless other communities around the world have persisted throughout history. Stereotypes happen when a group of people is characterized as having the same behaviors, physical attributes, and socioeconomic status. Stereotypes can turn dangerous when they are used to prove how one group is superior to others. At their extreme, they can lead to mass murder, as was the case in the 1930s and 1940s with Jewish people and other groups who didn't fit into the Nazi ideal of a pure race. The fake news of these racial stereotypes fueled the **Holocaust.** The constant propaganda

A 1940s book titled *Der Untermensch* ("the subhuman" in German) featured harsh photography meant to make readers fearful of Jewish people.

and fake news made people believe that anyone who did not support the Nazi cause was less than human.

Just two years after World War II (1939–45), fake news became a common exchange between the United States and the Union of Soviet Socialist Republics (Soviet Union). So began the Cold War (1947–91). Fake news grew because the Soviet Union wanted to establish Communist governments, and the United States worried that these Communist governments would spread into Western Europe and America. The propagandic talk of how dangerous the "other side" was fueled decades of tension between the United States and the Soviet Union.

The Soviet Union waged a propaganda campaign in the 1950s against the West, which included Allied powers from World War II such as the United States and Great Britain. Its national newspaper, *Pravda*, depicted the United States as a country of warmongers. It told Soviet citizens that they had been duped (much like Hitler had told the German people after World War I) into accepting a harsh post-war peace settlement that was not fair to their country. However, instead of using articles, pamphlets, and posters that depicted racial stereotypes, the Soviet government pushed the idea of nuclear bombs. It tried to convince citizens that they needed to protect themselves against warmongering America.

ZOOM IN: DENIAL RUNS DEEP

The more fake news there is, the more people tend to believe it. In 1969, a Washington, D.C., group called the Liberty Lobby began publishing literature that denied the Holocaust had ever happened. Noontide Press, a supporter of Liberty Lobby, published a book called *The Myth of the Six Million* to deny that the Nazis had killed so many Jews. A sensationalized cycle of circular reasoning grew from these initial fake news publications. Today, many Holocaust deniers have lost their following. In some countries, they've also lost lawsuits or been convicted of crimes for their actions. Yet this fake news story continues to live on the Internet and in print.

A Cold War-era Soviet propaganda cartoon portrayed the United States as a war-hungry country that would use nuclear bombs to take over the world.

The United States fought back with their own campaign against the Communists, often called "Reds." Posters said that Communism was America's mortal enemy. They showed images of Soviet leader Joseph Stalin clutching a globe in his arms and people running away from him in great fear. People tend to believe propaganda when they are afraid or confused, feelings that were common in post-World War II countries. The fear of Communists overtaking the United States led to investigations into supposed Communist spies in the

Senator Joseph McCarthy used television appearances to raise fear and suspicion in U.S. citizens, resulting in his own fame and power.

ZOOM IN: PERFECT WORLD

Along with paper propaganda, film footage was a way for Hitler and the Nazi Party to dehumanize Jewish people and spread lies. They also used it to give German people a sensationalized view of what life would be like in a "pure" world. The most popular of these films was *The Triumph of the Will.* Released in 1935, the same year enforcement of racial laws began in Germany, the film painted a celebratory picture of the Nazi Party. It showed young children and families happily interacting with the Nazis, who would ultimately be responsible for the deaths of six million Jews and millions of others.

U.S. government, as well as in news outlets, the entertainment industry, schools, and neighborhoods. People became leery of each other with so much propaganda swirling around them.

U.S. senator Joseph McCarthy was a leader in these spy campaigns. He accused more than 200 Americans of being Communists. In 1953, he started investigating the Army Signal Corps laboratory at Fort Monmouth, New Jersey, looking for Communist spies. Nothing was proven. McCarthy was seen as a bully for his questioning tactics. In response to McCarthy's continual screaming at witnesses and attacking the Army's credibility in the courtroom, the Army's appointed lawyer, Joseph N. Welch, said, "Until this moment, Senator, I think I never really gauged your cruelty or recklessness. . . . Have you no sense of decency, sir, at long last?" The trial did not end in McCarthy's favor.

Edward R. Murrow took a risk and reported about the rise of Communist accusations and McCarthy's tactics. On April 6, 1954, McCarthy appeared on Murrow's news show, *See It Now,* denouncing Murrow's objective reporting. Eventually, it was revealed that McCarthy's accusations were not true. He was reprimanded, or censured, by his fellow senators that December by a vote of 67-22.

CHAPTER 3:

Fake, Fake, Fake

It's January 2020. People are catching the bus or hopping the train to work. They're boarding airplanes and cruise ships. Others are filing into classrooms, offices, restaurants, or theaters. Life is "normal." But two months later, everything changes. In March, the United States locks down because of a virus called COVID-19. It's new, and there's no vaccine for it.

People start getting very sick. Some die. Hospital emergency rooms fill and overflow. Schools close. Many businesses close, while others scramble to find ways to deliver their goods contact-free. Soon, all types of stories flood the Internet. Social media quickly explodes with ideas on where the virus came from, who started it, and how a person can cure it. Some users claim COVID-19 is a **conspiracy** to take away people's rights, especially regarding wearing masks.

The COVID-19 virus was able to spread quickly around the globe because it was caught and carried by millions of airline travelers.

adidas
PIZZA GATE
IS REAL!

ZOOM IN: PIZZAGATE

In 2016, a conspiracy theory on social media said that supporters of Hilary Clinton and other Democrats were running a child sex-trafficking ring out of a Washington, D.C., pizzeria. The theory had a chilling effect on one man in particular who went so far as to drive to the pizzeria and start shooting people, to save the children. He was arrested and put in prison. In 2020, TikTok users who still believed the conspiracy called out businesspeople such as Bill Gates as perpetrators and celebrities such as Justin Bieber as victims. That year alone, TikTok posts for "Pizzagate" exceeded 82 million.

Although social media platforms were thick with falsehoods during the COVID-19 pandemic, they were also the only places people could socialize without fear of contracting the virus. Research data shows that there were three types of fake news running through the airwaves at the time: false claims, conspiracy theories, and **pseudoscientific** health therapies.

A false claim sounds like a fact but isn't. Some false claims said the virus could be spread by houseflies or mosquito bites. Others said it could be cured by drinking cow or camel urine. Other false claims said to inhale methanol vapor to combat the virus or use vodka as hand sanitizer. A conspiracy theory tends to envelop these types of false claims. One theory said that the virus was a "Chinese virus" intentionally spread by Chinese people. Another conspiracy theory said the virus was spread by 5G cellular network towers.

Pseudoscience is a false science based on false claims. For example, hot air blown up the nose is an unproven cure for COVID-19 based on non-expert advice. So is the claim that the pneumonia or malaria vaccine protects against it. These types of pseudoscience remedies usually help to promote conspiracy theories, such as the belief that all vaccinations are dangerous and should be avoided.

Fake news exploded with the rise of COVID-19. News changed every few hours on social media. People didn't know what to believe. Campaigning for the 2020 presidential election was happening at the same time and was done largely online. There was a deep divide along political lines about how to address the pandemic. Americans were tired, confused, and angry. Unrest boiled over following the killing of a Black man named George Floyd in Minneapolis, Minnesota. All summer, nationwide protests against police brutality and unjust treatment of people of color filled television and computer screens.

With tensions already high, Election Day came. After the vote on November 3, Americans anxiously waited for the results, many of which were announced prematurely on social media. On November 13, news channels confirmed that Joe Biden had won the 2020 presidential election. However, many supporters of President Trump did not agree with the results. They began spreading conspiracy theories online. They protested at polling places against the work of the election judges. The most prominent of the conspiracy theories fell on the work of the election judges in

TRUMP
-2020-
KEEP AMERICA GREAT!
TRUMP
CERTIFY
TRUMP

ZOOM IN: SPIES AND LIES

In the 1980s, a mysterious disease called AIDS (acquired immunodeficiency syndrome) struck the world hard. As scientists raced to figure out its cause and how it was spread, many people fell victim to conspiracy theories. In 1985, an article written by German biologist Jakob Segel suggested that military researchers at Maryland's Fort Detrick had accidentally spread the virus through experiments on prison inmates. This theory was later proved to be part of a misinformation campaign by the Soviet spy agency known as the KGB.

Georgia. The judges were accused of either counting extra votes for Biden or not counting all the votes for Trump.

Fake news about the presidential election ran rampant for weeks. As the day of Biden's inauguration approached, conspiracy theories about a "stolen election" were common. One conspiracy video by NewsMax was shared more than 350,000 times on Facebook. The stories confused people. Which sources were real and which were fake?

On January 6, 2021, protestors attacked the U.S. Capitol, claiming that the 2020 presidential election was rigged. At his own rally, Trump told the crowd, "We're going to the Capitol. We're going to try and give them [Republicans] the kind of pride and boldness they need to take back this country." Trump never went to the Capitol, but large crowds of his supporters did.

As protestors chanted for Trump in front of the U.S. Capitol, rioters broke windows and doors. They forced their way into the offices of government officials and posted photos of their achievements on social media. Some rioters made their way into the U.S. Senate chamber. Senators sought safety wherever they could. The chaos lasted for hours, until the National Guard arrived and teamed with Capitol police to bring peace to the area. Seven people died in connection with the January 6 attack, including Capitol police officer Brian Sicknick. Many who were involved in what is now known as the "January 6 Insurrection" faced federal charges on multiple crimes.

The stolen election claims weren't the first or last claims of fake news Trump made. One of the first times he used the term "fake news" was in 2017, when referring to Cable News Network (CNN). These claims gained traction during the 2016 presidential election campaign, with the social media platform Twitter playing a star role. Just a month before the 2016 election, there were 6.6 million tweets linked to fake news and conspiracy news stories. Many fake accounts on social media helped to spread fake news and bully social media users into believing the lies.

This surge in social media exploited users without the media literacy to separate truth from dis- or misinformation. Many older users expected social media sites to follow the same guidelines and practices employed by the traditional news sources they had grown up with. When social media, especially Facebook, increased the spread of false information, these users were unable to tell the difference. They believed they could trust what was published, but the news they read wasn't true in the first place.

CHAPTER 4:

Critical Thinking

Why do people believe fake news? In the 1970s, psychologists learned that even if a person knew a story was false, they would believe it, as long as it validated that person's **bias** or idea.

According to Norbert Schwarz, a professor of psychology and marketing at the University of Southern California, people tend to use five things to calculate if something is true: 1) Compatibility with other known information; 2) Credibility of the source; 3) Whether others believe it; 4) Whether the information is internally consistent; and 5) Whether there is supporting evidence.

Critical thinking skills play a key role in understanding information and our own leanings toward certain ideas, even if an idea may not be objectively true. For example, studies show that people tend to be more skeptical of ideas that do not align with their political beliefs. This type of skeptical thinking becomes dangerous

As more people consume information on their smartphones, they will need critical thinking skills to determine the accuracy of what they read and see.

Author Eli Saslow

ZOOM IN: CHANGING COURSE

Growing up, Derek Black, son of longtime white nationalist celebrity Don Black, believed the same things his father believed. He believed immigration was bad and that the white race needed to be preserved. At college, Derek ran a white nationalist radio show in the morning and attended classes afterward. He began having conversations with members of the Jewish community, Black community, and other groups of color—the exact people he was advocating against. These "quiet conversations" led Black to question his ideas about race and eventually change course. His story is the subject of Pulitzer-prize winning journalist Eli Saslow's book *Rising Out of Hatred: The Awakening of a Former White Nationalist.*

when people start to create ideas not based on facts, leading to larger conspiracies and division among groups of people.

Researchers define critical thinking as taking the time to question and analyze information in an un-biased way to make reasoned decisions. Critical thinking is an important part of learning, reading, and understanding the world around us. Our critical thinking skills can help us step back from the emotional pull of a story and look at the facts. We can double-check those facts by talking with others and seeing what other information is out there.

When we think critically, we can better analyze information for its motives or intentions. This is where the terms misinformation, disinformation, and mal-information come in. Misinformation is false information shared with no intention of causing harm to others—a simple misunderstanding. Disinformation is false information shared with the intent to cause harm to others. This includes conspiracies spread online about different groups of people. Mal-information is true information shared with the intent to cause harm. Cyberbullying often includes mal-information.

Federal and state governments recognize that fake news is a problem. President Biden and his administration publicly called out Russian propaganda news outlets for spreading disinformation about the 2022 invasion of Ukraine. To combat child pornography and political misinformation, Minnesota's government passed a bill in 2023 that made it a crime to solicit **deepfakes**. Deepfakes are falsified videos that usually swap people's characteristics to show them as a real part of a made-up video. These videos have been a large part of the fake news world in the past decade.

Social media platforms have beefed up their efforts to stop fake news as well. After the intense rise of fake news following the 2016 presidential election, Facebook took down what it thought were fake accounts, tightened its misinformation policies, and showcased an ad database that promoted transparency. After the January 6 Insurrection, Facebook and Twitter suspended President Trump's accounts to stop any further calls to violence. However, some people saw these moves as contrary to U.S. citizens' right to free speech. They questioned the platforms' intentions and accused them of having political motives. Fake news continued to rise at an alarming rate.

In 2022, researchers found that 20 percent of the videos shared on the TikTok platform were spreading misinformation to its mostly younger audience. Twitter laid off many employees in 2022 and 2023, as did Google, who owns YouTube. Included in the layoffs were policy experts who handled misinformation.

USA
THANK YOU TOUR 2016
Hershey, Pennsylvania
MAKE AMERICA GREAT AGAIN

Although most of the policies designed to fight fake news are still in place, the resources needed to enforce them have decreased. Researchers disagree on how effective the policies are because the fake news content may still be shared, but others feel having rules and regulations is a step in the right direction.

Researchers do agree that the best way to combat fake news is to encourage professional news reporting and for governments to set good examples for other countries to follow. News organizations need to work together to call out fake news. People can also look to independent, neutral nonprofit organizations such as Snopes and Politifact to help combat fake news when they question a story.

Researchers do agree that the best way to combat fake news is to encourage professional news reporting and for governments to set good examples for other countries to follow.

Fake news has become a part of everyday life in the United States. It spreads quickly on social media, leading to circular reasoning reporting, which never allows for the development of a full story, which takes days—even months—for facts to fully emerge. Technology will continue to advance, but the news needs to stay real. When you see a news story, use your critical thinking skills. Ask questions before sharing it. Does the story come from a credible source? Who sent the information? Don't share on impulse. Stop and breathe first. Are you sharing the news because it's true or because it plays to your emotions by making you angry or scared? Learn about tools that can help verify images and videos, trust scientists before politicians, and know what you don't know. Take time away from the screen to talk with your teachers, mentors, friends, and family about ideas you see that sound confusing or questionable. These conversations will not only help stop the spread of fake news, but they will help you learn about other people and communities, too.

ZOOM IN: STAYING IN CHECK

Snopes is the oldest and largest fact-checking website in the world. It first appeared in 1994, investigating hoaxes and random urban legends. Snopes staff members take news stories and research them to make sure the facts are correct. They are successful because of their ability to be independent of news channels and other media. Users can search Snopes for the latest news developments, the top current rumors, and archived articles about crime, the paranormal, and more. In the first month of the COVID-19 pandemic, more than 36 million people visited the Snopes website.

Getting Real

MARTHA ROUNDTREE

Meet the Press is the longest running program in television history. Pioneer journalist Martha Roundtree was its first host. She was also the only woman to moderate it, until Kristen Welker came aboard in 2023. For years, the show has been a huge success because of its tough questions and panelist discussions across the political spectrum. Even though not everyone agrees on the show, everyone agrees to talk with each other about greater ideas for the nation. Roundtree once said about the show, "I think it is important that the public should hear its elected officials speak out and take their stand in answer to direct questions, without preparation." The panel format continues to be successful on the show and countless other TV news shows.

Roundtree first arrived in New York City in 1938. She worked as a freelance writer and became friends with Lawrence E. Spivak. Together, they started *Meet the Press* on the radio, in 1945. Two years later, they launched the show on television. Roundtree sold her share of the show to Spivak in a coin toss in 1953 and went on to further her career.

She produced other television and radio shows, including *Leave It to the Girls*, which was radio's first panel show in 1945. She also produced *Keep Posted*, *Washington Exclusive*, *Press Conference*, and *Capital Close-Up*. Roundtree won a Peabody Award in 1952 for her journalistic excellence and contributions to the field. Roundtree was well known for her creative spirit and generous giving. She died in 1999 at the age of 87.

SANDER VAN DER LINDEN

Sander van der Linden, PhD, is a professor of social psychology in society at the University of Cambridge in the United Kingdom. He's also the director of the Cambridge Social Decision-Making Lab. With his colleague Jon Roozenbeek, PhD, van der Linden developed two different interactive Internet games to help people combat fake news: *Bad News* and *Go Viral!*

Bad News is a game that simulates how people can gain followers through social media and how fake news can spread. It's quick and fun for any age. In *Go Viral!*, players choose an avatar and walk in the shoes of a social media manipulator. It shows players how different types of posts are more manipulative than factual.

Van der Linden believes there are six types of manipulation tactics used to spread fake news: impersonating things, creating a conspiracy, playing with people's emotions, polarizing a group, discrediting others, and trolling people. Van der Linden is passionate about combating misinformation in the United States. He continues to work with the World Health Organization (WHO), the United Nations, and the United Kingdom Cabinet Office to fight fake news. His new book, *Foolproof: Why Misinformation Infects Our Minds and How to Build Immunity,* was released in 2023. Kirkus Reviews gave it a starred review, stating that the book is "[a] well-researched, psychologically astute book . . . and a powerful argument for the effectiveness of delivering a small dose of misinformation in order to inoculate against a major infection . . . insightful, convincing, instructive reading."

Timeline

1780s

Gossip columns become a normal part of newspapers.

1782

Benjamin Franklin creates a fake issue of the *Boston Newspaper* to build support for the American Revolution.

1835

The *New York Sun* runs the "Great Moon Hoax" as a strategy to draw in more readers.

1844

Anti-Catholic newspapers falsely accuse Irishmen of robbing schools and stealing Bibles, sparking the Philadelphia Bible Riots.

1915

Fake news about a German "corpse factory" spreads through newspapers worldwide.

1924–53

Communist leaders spread disinformation and prompt Senator Joseph McCarthy to start an extreme campaign against possible Communist supporters in the United States.

1938

Listeners miss a disclaimer before a radio performance of *The War of the Worlds* and panic, thinking Martians are attacking Earth.

1933–45

Under Hitler's leadership, Nazi propaganda spreads against Jews and other groups.

1983

An article circulates that falsely says AIDS started at the Pentagon as a U.S. experiment.

1991

A rumor claims that former Soviet leader Vladimir Lenin's body will be auctioned off for millions of dollars.

2016

The conspiracy #Pizzagate falsely accuses U.S. presidential candidate Hilary Clinton of running a child-trafficking ring.

2017

A longtime neo-Nazi website is taken offline for a month because of its message of hate.

2020

As COVID-19 spreads, 582 fake news stories are debunked by fact-checkers in the first month alone.

2021

Facebook bars President Trump and Twitter suspends his account for his role in the January 6 U.S. Capitol attack.

2022

A conspiracy theory claims that people with COVID-19 will get monkey pox.

Glossary

bias—an inclination or leaning towards an idea or prejudice

broadcast news—a medium in broadcasting news events and other information through the electronic means, such as radio, television, or Internet

circular reasoning—a way to say an opinion is true because another source says it is true

colonial—period of settlement in North America from the 1600s through the late 1700s

conspiracy—a secret plan with unlawful or evil intent

critical thinking—ability to think clearly and rationally

deepfake—a falsified video or video image

hoax—a deception with various intentions, such as malicious or humorous

Holocaust—the systemic mass murder of the Jews by the Nazi regime during WWII

literacy—ability to read and write

media—forms of mass communication, including online newspapers, broadcast news, and social networking sites like TikTok, Facebook, and Instagram

propaganda—misleading information used to promote or publicize a particular ideology, political cause, or point of view

pseudoscientific—falsely or mistakenly being claimed as scientific evidence

sensationalism—the use of exciting or shocking stories, whether true or not, to provoke public interest and excitement

stereotype—a widely held, fixed idea about something that is usually oversimplified and/or disrespectful

Selected Bibliography

Hasen, Richard L. *Cheap Speech: How Disinformation Poisons Our Politics—and How to Cure It.* New Haven, Conn.; London: Yale University Press, 2022.

Levitin, Daniel J. *Weaponized Lies: How to Think Critically in the Post-Truth Era.* New York: Dutton, 2016.

Naím, Moisés. *The Revenge of Power: How Autocrats Are Reinventing Politics for the 21st Century.* New York: St. Martin's Press, 2022.

O'Connor, Cailin, and James Owen Weatherall. *The Misinformation Age: How False Beliefs Spread.* New Haven, Conn.: Yale University Press, 2019.

Rid, Thomas. *Active Measures: The Secret History of Disinformation and Political Warfare.* New York: Farrar, Straus and Giroux, 2020.

Schwartz, A. Brad. *Broadcast Hysteria: Orson Welles's War of the Worlds and the Art of Fake News.* New York: Hill and Wang, 2015.

Van der Linden, Sander. *Foolproof: Why Misinformation Infects Our Minds and How to Build Immunity.* New York: W. W. Norton & Company, 2023.

Websites

Britannica: Propaganda
https://www.britannica.com/topic/propaganda

Explore the subject of propaganda and its role in fake news.

FactCheck.org
https://www.factcheck.org

A nonpartisan site that verifies facts stated by key players in U.S. politics.

Westchester Community College: Real News vs. Fake News
https://library.sunywcc.edu/fakenews

Learn about fake news, how to spot it, and why you should care about it.

Index